FAMILIAR SPIRITS

Also by Elizabeth Jennings
from Carcanet

Collected Poems
Selected Poems
Tributes
Times and Seasons

Elizabeth Jennings

FAMILIAR SPIRITS

CARCANET

for Robert Ombres O.P.

First published in 1994 by
Carcanet Press Limited
208-212 Corn Exchange Buildings
Manchester M4 3BQ

A CIP catalogue record for this book
is available from the British Library.
ISBN 1 85754 091 3

The publisher acknowledges financial assistance
from the Arts Council of England

Set in 10pt Palatino by Bryan Williamson, Frome
Printed and bound in England by SRP Ltd, Exeter

Contents

The World We Made	7
The First Music	9
An Uncle and Godfather	10
Our Maids	11
Slow Movement: Autumn	12
A Cliff Walk in North Devon when I was Twelve	13
Sky in Childhood	14
Camp	15
First Love	16
A Way to Imagine	17
My Father's Father	18
Blood Bonds, Family Feelings	19
Cousins, Aunts, Uncles	20
Old Friends	21
A Realisation	22
A Coffee House	23
Bicycles in Summer	24
Sea Music	25
Among the Stars	26
It is not True?	27
Cities: Their Beginning	29
Unto the Hills	30
Love Whispered	31
Almost	32
Squares and Circles	33
Genes, Likenesses	34
After a Film called *The Bridge*	35
September	37
Still Life	38
The Roots	39
Overture to Spring	40
Steps Towards Poems	41
Passed Down	42
Unsaid	43
Katie: A Portrait	44
In Praise of Anonymity	45
'Music of the Spheres'	46
Two Sonnets on Love and Lust	47
For Louise Aged 12, My Great-Niece	48
My Sister	49

Death of a Father who was a Poet   50
A Very Great Friend and Influence   51
Fables, Lessons   54
The Modes of Love
    In Love   55
    Lullaby for Lovers   56
    Contradictions   57
    The Test   58
    Obsessive Love   59
    Over   60
    Lust   61
    Married Love   62
    Friendship   63
    The Seer's Love   64

The World We Made

We were aware of everything but ourselves,
    Listened, watched and thought
We did everything totally, never by halves,
    Intricate kingdoms were wrought

By the network and depth of our imagination.
    Everything that we saw
Or heard or touched or smelt was part of a passion
    And we were alert to awe.

One day we put a little cochineal
    Into an eggcup and
From it made a world which was more real
    Than the one which was close at hand.

The god we worshipped we named Cochineal
    And he was a Sun God.
We shaped a totem pole and painted all
    The angriest things we could

Think of on it – red faces, skulls and knives
    And round it we danced, of course.
Upon such games as this a childhood thrives
    And builds up such a force

Of memories, foretellings, wise delights.
    Everything had a place
In our dervish dances, our cardboard swords, our rites
    And all had an odd grace.

Maybe because order was everywhere
    Nothing was meaningless
But my father was troubled and one day said, 'You are
    Christians, you know.' His distress

Was something that we could not understand
    Yet trespassing on our world
He had overshadowed and spoilt it for us and
    Our fervour soon grew cold.

Our Sun God stayed in the sky and somehow had
    Lost most of its power.
Of course we were grateful for it when it shed
    Its heat upon us but our

Religion had foundered on what we did not know
    Was called reality then.
We forgot our dances and rites and started to grow
    Like the dullard rest of men.

The world outside us hadn't changed but we
    Found imagination was
Something to do with art and poetry.
    Our great world came to a close.

Cochineal was drawn back to a bottle
    Of colouring essence, our pole
Was lost in an attic while we ourselves had to settle
    Down in a world not whole

Or satisfying or orderly while we
    Shrank into teenagers who,
Conscious of little but themselves, aren't free
    To dream but must learn to know.

The First Music

What was the first music
After the chirping of birds, the barking of foxes
After the hoot of owls, the mooing of cows,
The murmur of dawn birds, winds in the trees?
Did all these tell the first men they must make
Their own music? Mothers would lullaby
Their babies to sleep, warriors certainly shouted.
But what was the first music that was its own
Purpose, a pattern or phrasing, a quality
Of sound that came between silences and cast out
All other possible sounds? It must have been man
Singing in love and exultation, hearing
The high sweet song of blackbirds. When did he fashion
A harp or horn? O how much I would give
To hear that first and pristine music and know
That it changed the turning planet and visited stars.

An Uncle and Godfather

Uncle and godfather, how patiently
You read my early poems. You were upon
My level too for your attentive mind
You gladly brought to bear on every one
Of my young verses, called them poetry.

All those ambitious ballads, sonnets, odes
Which I most valued you would read but yet
Told me a four-line poem which was based
Upon a dead bird I held in my hand,
Was in your careful judgment far the best.

Slightly disappointed at the time,
I knew when I grew up that you were right.
You showed me truth's the heart of poetry.
I owe so much to your clear, kind insight.
I learnt from you that rhythm, form and rhyme

Are at the service of what's deeper – craft
Was an essential to all poems. You had
Once published a small volume of your verse
And lent your findings to a small child's gift.
Today imagination throngs my head

As it did once but discipline also
Curbs and refines it. This you taught to me
And never told me how bad most poems were
When I first wrote them. You saw poetry
Was present in those four lines and would grow.

Our Maids

Our maids did not have names like my friends' names.
    How snobbish that seems now!
Sometimes they joined me in my private games
I never knew that they had not known how

It feels to be a child until eighteen.
    Elsie stole and I
Recall my mother saying it had been
Hard to sack her. She saw Elsie cry

But I did not. Lily Lovegrove had
    Strange habits. Now and then
She'd have a fit of rage when she felt bad
And used to slam all doors, but always when

She had a holiday she'd bring us back
    Kind presents, sweets and toys.
She'd never known her parents yet the lack
Had left her generous. When she talked of boys

She never said that she had been admired.
    A child easily
Accepts the strange, the odd. I never tired
Of simple stories Lily told to me.

Then there was Ivy. Ivy got the sack
    For seeming to pollute
My mind although I did not know it. Back
My mother sent her, said 'she did not suit'.

And so when I was six or seven I had
    Learnt much about odd ways.
Not one of our maids had been really bad.
How wrong for them – and us – were those 'old days'.

Slow Movement: Autumn

Falling, golden falling of brown leaves,
Slow sunsets, still long days though they diminish,
A time of memory of childhood years
And picking blackberries, I now remember,
And dreading school. O treacherous September,
I cling to you as leaves do to the branch
Until a long, slow wind insists they go.
Mid-August's summer still but at its end
Days grow a little shorter. Every year
In August I am moved back to the time
Of school's commencement. How I used to fear
Cold mornings and bleak lessons. Then began
A melancholy never known before,
Sadness which only those who've been in love
Understand fully. Yes, a touch of sadness
Came to me in September every year
And it's grown into me, is now a habit
So that I dread a non-existent school
And long-gone lessons every new September.
O falling season, autumn sadness, use
Sounds like the touch of bows on violins
Moving within me, telling me once again
About the autumn and how it begins.

A Cliff Walk in North Devon when I was Twelve

I was walking along a cliff,
It was late afternoon and a cool wind blew my hair,
Below was the casual sea in its commotions,
In and out, out and in as if
It would catch out the very tides.
I could see the wet sand and slowly appearing pools
Where my grandfather caught netfuls of prawns while we,
My sister and I, caught four or five between us.
But that day I was happy alone and walking along
The high cliff. I breathed the healing salt,
Stared at the sea moving and suddenly had
Such a sense of exaltation,
Such certainty that all was well with the world
And I was one with, at ease with everything,
Reconciled to the humdrum hurts of life,
Knowing for certain that some invisible Power
Had fashioned the turning seas and the tides and moon
And made me for some purpose as yet unknown
But something, however small or large it was,
Only I could achieve but need not hurry.
No, must not hurry but move in accord with tide,
Collecting the changing moons, being grateful and glad
That for a moment or two I could see creation
Planned and purposed and somehow achieved by love.

Sky in Childhood

A child, I watched the sky and said 'Up there'
  And 'there' meant Heaven for me.
I could imagine saints, long row on row
  And angels' minstrelsy.

Grown-up, I read of aeons away and of
  Star beyond star beyond star.
Yet this says nothing of my God-man's love,
  It only causes fear

And vertigo. Last night I thought of this
  And strangely once again
I thought of angels and of Mary's love
  For her new baby. His

Power holds every star within its place
  And all the energy
That causes every cell to move, since grace
  Is vaster than gravity,

More wonderful than any star or sky
  And just as bright to see.
Near Christmas now one star is breaking free
  And all grace is nearby,

Ready for us to take and feel delight.
  Heavenly star, you show
Time does not matter on this holy night.
  Man's spirit is aglow

And there is surely 'music of the spheres'
  If we will only keep
Silent for it to drive away our fears
  And orchestrate our sleep.

Camp

We catch up with emotions later on,
    Those of childhood I mean,
My first rejection by a friend is one
Of these. My memory holds the time and scene.

A child of twelve, I went to camp because
    A friend insisted I
Should go. When we arrived she quickly was
Off with another girl. I hid to cry

For it's a rule at school that you don't sneak
    About your hurts but my
Sister found me. School codes let you break
The rules when blood's the bond. I was told I

Could go into my sister's tent but with
    An acted courage then
I turned that down. Still, trust had found its death
And I know now it could not live again.

First Love

Does it die wholly, that first love which is
    So selfless and so pure?
It does not ask for reciprocity's
Proud demands but worships from afar

And asks for nothing. Yet it alters all
    You were and makes you grow.
This surely was man's love before the Fall.
It teaches happiness you did not know

Was possible. I can remember how
    A school-friend said to me,
'Emma likes you.' It comes ringing now.
That love which bound and yet meant liberty.

A Way to Imagine

I painted a house that morning
I coated the walls with yellow stucco and how
The sun made friends with it,
I painted the door dark green and the window shutters
Sported the same colour.
I planted a white rose to climb that yellow wall
And placed a fountain eight yards from the door.
I looked at the huge sun and the blazing blue
Of the hot Summer sky,
I heard some children singing but could not see them,
I heard a blackbird singing with happiness.
I saw the house owner drive away in his car,
I dipped my hands in the fountain's pool and then
Took one more look at that delightful house
And with scores of birdsong breaking upon my ears
I walked through the front door.

My Father's Father

I never met my father's father who
    Died in his fifties when
I was very small, say one or two;
Later my mother said he was a man

Of gentleness whose presence filled a house
    With comfort and with peace,
He never lost his temper or let loose
Disappointment. He put all at ease.

I wish I could remember all of this.
    His wife was different.
She lived with us for years, would nag at us
And often spoiled my mother's happiness.

She seldom was upset but one day I
    Saw her at the door
And she was obviously about to cry
And run away. My father stopped her there.

But she adored his father, loved to have
    Him staying with us. How
I wished that I had known his gentle love
And, so much later, wish it even now.

Blood Bonds, Family Feelings

It's in the blood and yet it is much more.
It's sympathy and pride. It will not have
A sharer criticised. It is a shore
On which encroaches one huge body of
Power reined in and then released. This love

Fits no one definition yet it grows
As bodies do. Its spirit is the way
Gifts are repeated, looks are shared. It knows
The constant ebb and flow of amity.
Loose anger on one member and it shows

Immediate alliance. I recall
Childhood moments when my sister would
Boss me about and yet would never fail,
When others criticised, to be my good
Defence, a kind ghost in my neighbourhood.

Cousins, Aunts, Uncles

Not close enough for vows or bitter words
Yet near enough for family blood to matter –
I think of those my cousins I've not seen
　　　For years, and some not ever,
And wonder, if we met, our family cords
Would bring us near at once, or maybe never.

I do not think embarrassment would make
A barrier yet maybe guilt would find
A place, some guilt I mean that we have stayed
　　　So far apart. Maybe
There would not be a sense of 'old time's sake'
Or merely wonder that our family

So large in number never has been close.
The only aunt I really felt near to
Died first of all the family although
　　　She was the fourth of eight,
A loving humour rose in both of us.
Maybe for all new meetings it's too late.

My mother died two years ago when I
Was ill and so not at her funeral.
Her nature knew no bitterness, was kind
　　　But sensitive and shy,
Childlike and gentle. She would always find

Intrinsic worth in people. If she were
Alive today I think that she would bring
Us all together, uncles, cousins, aunts
　　　For she would keep in touch
With all the family. If she were here
Today, each one of us would be in reach.

Old Friends

We are children still to one another
    In what we say and don't,
Closer than blood-bonds ours seem and together
We enter many worlds as was our wont,

We speak a language that is private and
    With it enter places
Few of our relatives can understand.
We find in friendship many kinds of graces

Which passion can know nothing of because
    The flesh is so strong there.
Yet some too of the sweetness which love knows
Moves around us like this summer air.

In such a season long ago we would
    Play our religious games.
We knew indeed the measure of our God,
Yet worshipped him and gave him many names.

Now through five decades we have come again
    After lost years, O yes.
But now upon our friendship there's no stain
And we together shape a steadfastness

For as we talk of 'making friends' so do
    We make a mood and home
Which can surprise us sometimes and be new.
We mint gold wisdom for our friendship's sum.

A Realisation

It is only today that I
Have suddenly thought that I have no-one who
    Cares for me totally,
No-one to whom I come first. There are a few
    Who think of me, certainly,

But there is no longer one
To whom I am the world, the centre, the heart,
    The headstrong noonday sun,
And of course I too love many who play a part
    In my universe, but gone

Are the one or two I've known
With whom I broke the Galilean claim.
    Who were the suns which spun
About my earth. Yes, I have none to name
    For whom I'm the only one.

A Coffee House

A little boy of twenty months. He fits
Exactly into space and floor.
He runs a few yards as his mother sits
Talking but she's soon after him. What's more

She wears an anxious frown. He's full of glee
Not knowing how we all
Share in watching over him while he
Laughs loudly. He knows he will not fall

Although he hasn't moved about for long –
Fair hair, a smile of grace.
If he knew one he'd sing a morning call
But there is worry on each watching face

For this year one horrific murder was
Done by two boys of ten.
Our minds are full of that and all its loss.
When shall we laugh with children once again?

You could not go today. It is not safe.
I mean those summer afternoons when we
Left home at two on bicycles to go
Through lanes, along the highways, then beneath
Deep dark of oak and chestnut. We rode with
Absolute confidence, alert to all
We saw. We took our swimming things and buns,
Bottles of lemonade, our port of call
A Norman church lit now and then by sun's
Reach through the leaves. Then on and on we went
Not saying much, in pleasant mood. We would
Undress beside the Cherwell or the Thames,
Both unpolluted, and jump in and swim,
Splash and go beneath the water's surface
To glimpse the sun's fall, then reach up and out,
Rubbing ourselves with towels, on bikes again.
It was a pastoral childhood that we knew
A child can't have today. It is not safe
To let our children out alone for hours
Like two to seven. Darkness falls at noon,
The dark of roaming men intent on crime
But we were lucky in our summer days,
Lucky in losing every sense of time,
Lucky in feeling warm from towels and sun,
Loving old churches, following the Thames,
Learning the world by love and childhood games.

Sea Music

How to catch it, how to find the deep
Accurate notes, how to show the way salt smells
And how the tide drags and raises, pulls down
And then lifts up and curls and falls and slides
Like snow beneath skis, like agile drifts
Of some crêpe-de-chine falling over and down.

Can anyone catch for mind or instrument every
Tension and release, every gesture and slow
Kind movement? O I watched it for an hour
Thinking of last night's moon and finding it hard
To believe that power and invisible plucking. Tide
Was coming in, dragging the sea over shingle,
Riding over every rock-pool, recording
Its echo music. I think I almost had
The right word then but it slipped from my mind
Though music was all about in its own order.
I listened entranced, I stared at the ruled horizon
Knowing the notes were falling out of hearing
And that I would never find orchestral words
Or catch the sea though I was near it in childhood
Standing on breakwaters, paddling in the rock-pools,
My mind at one with the tangy exuberant air
And the heady, salt-laden breakers climbing around me.

Among the Stars

I walked into our garden one spring night,
    Warmth moved among the trees,
The stars were plentiful and in their light
I felt an exaltation such as is

Offered at times but never earned. I was
    Caught by a wonder which
I'd never heard of. Now it is a grace,
That night the very Heavens seemed to reach

Down to my stance. My spirit and my flesh
    Were one existence then.
How often since has such joy been my wish
As then was granted to a child of ten.

It is not True?

It comes to me at midnight it is true
We don't believe in death. It can't be so
Or not for those we know as me and you.

It is a state, a happening, an event
For those who're strangers to us. Death is meant
For others. In newspapers in dark print

We read of great ones going. We think of
The fact a moment, then turn back to love
And care and all the ways that we must move

To work, to play, while death goes on elsewhere.
It is a message carried through the air,
Something that happened when we were not there.

But wait, a day arrives when someone close
Is taken ill and dies. We feel the loss
And thoughts of our own deaths return to us.

My mother died two years ago today.
I often think of questions I could say
That only she could answer. She's away

But where and how? O love, we quarrel and
Neither will speak. Then one puts out a hand
The other takes. We start to understand

Our final goings and we are afraid
And I, not you, believe we are not made
To go forever. When we often said

Death is not true, I think we were in part
Precisely right. When we make works of art
We think they'll last. O when did mankind start

To think of death as somehow to begin
Our lives a different way, to start again
And live life flawlessly? Our minds move in

Countries untried but waiting for us. Love
Conjures up lands which death knows nothing of
And forevers are convincing proof,

And hint at lastings. Love goes further still,
Suggesting we have spirits death can't kill.
O love I am afraid of this as well.

Cities: Their Beginning

First it is a city of the heart.
In some far-back imagining there is
A place to wonder at, to stroll through and
To be acquainted with great craft and art.
Cities are places makers understand,
     And so from fantasies

A real place is built. The architects
Consider light and shade, the climate too.
Dreams are drawn down to possibilities
And men consider little human acts
And needs. The greatest cities always please
     But must be makeshift too.

For we, the dwellers, are untidy and
Wreckers also. We are proud to see
The spires and towers, pigeon-haunted squares,
But we are not designed and never planned
Except in minds of wise men who split hairs,
     Yet sometimes we can be

Visionaries for an hour or two,
And in those hours our spirits rise to heights
And show our city is a magic place.
And it is then that artists have to show
Order, renewal, moments filled with grace.
     It's in moon-flooded nights

That now and then we fit our aspirations.
Children are lullabied, quiet love is made
And windows are flung open to the stars.
Cities then fit our bold imaginations
And in the symphony of distant cars
     Our souls are strings well-played.

Unto the Hills

Mountains for wise men – how I see them glow.
With good red sky at night their peaks are crowned.
Moses and Jesus have climbed, lesser men too.
What throngs of thought have risen from the ground,
    What findings of what's true.

Is it coolness which refreshes minds?
'Mine eyes are lifted up', I understand
That in heights of cloud or mountain I may find
Peace and wisdom. Spring is close at hand,
    Whose light clears and can blind.

Love Whispered

Love whispered to the tide-out
And sang across the wet, reflecting sand.
We were holding hands and murmuring not words
But sounds of supplication, lyric graces.

I have learnt all this from the ocean
In lessons of tide-in and tide-out
As I think myself back to first childhood
And beyond that to floating in kind water
And love that made me and launched me
Into the salt seas of now.

Almost

It almost was not. That is what I say
About this minute coloured by the sea,
About this chestnut losing its huge hands
About the boys who pick the polished conkers.
This almost was not now and setting sun
In pink surrenders, scarlet streaks foretelling
Good weather certainly. Now,
I celebrate the clothing of all these,
Their singing and their colour and this now
We stand in peacefully as night intrudes
In kind dark dusk. O celebrate with me.

Squares and Circles

I couldn't paint it that day
Nor the next nor the next nor the next
But on one clear winter morning
I saw my scene of September
In bars of light and squares of yellow
And dizzying circles of red and orange
I quickly opened my paint-box
And put down the colours exactly
And in between the circles and squares
Smiling children were shouting,
Laughing and playing with shadows
Just outside my picture.

Genes, Likenesses

What is this in me called spirit or
Soul or being, self which I call me?
So many qualities I owe to more
Than one ancestor but my self is free
Of them. It knows of law

And duty, choice, responsibility,
Yet it is dressed in clothes much like those of
Some member of my huge past family
And closer ones whom I know best through love,
And then there's liberty

Whose boundaries are often hard to know.
My voice, my eyes, my hair, my shape of head
Are easy likenesses to see although
They are so mingled, but my present need
Moves further, deeper too.

My spirit's part of my imagination
And also part of thought and memory.
Then there are ways of feeling, also passion.
Can spirits look alike? Is soul not free
To be unique and its own revelation?
I say my history's me.

After a Film called The Bridge

he looked at the forms
            and colours of the
                        young woman
                  standing on a
                              bridge
she turned her head and
                  he looked at her
                              with passion
she was coy and twirled
                  her parasol
then turned her back
                  on him

in his sketch he jotted
                  down what the sun
                        showed
            which he would complete in oils
here were two sorts
            of desire
the painter's to capture
                  the roving sun on
                  a figure
and a man and a woman
                  held in a
                        different wish
      did they know even
                        then
            in a matter of only
                              seconds
that they must undress
            and lie in each other's
                        arms
part of this at least
            was gathering their
                        senses together
but he was seeing a
            woman in lights and
                              shadows
                  in circles
                        and squares

                              in glowings
          what would they do
                  when the sun went down
                              at last
          would they make love
          he would certainly one
                          day paint her
          the act of love seemed
                  part of the act
                          of creation
                  in colours upon a canvas
          the sea was coming in
                  I turned away
                like an intruder

September

When I woke up, the window
Showed me September, told me
Of crisp leaves being toasted,
Of days closing into their envelope,
The envelope placed on a table
As we thought of bed-time and children,
Here was a subject indeed.

but it isn't
the painter is playing
a very beautiful (usually)
trick. Think of Cézanne's *Apples*
or a narrow vase of flowers by Chardin
or a pair of old boots
by Van Gogh
who could also make you care for
a chair or a bed
long before Pop artists
or Op ones thought they were making
you look at a chair closely
simply by putting a solid one
on a very small platform
I won't say a 'real' one
because art is all an illusion
but a mysterious one that somehow
takes you to truth by imitation
because Cézanne's *apples*
and Van Gogh's *chair*
look utterly unlike
anything you have eaten
or sat on, and Chardin's vase of flowers
is his own, in his style
and that is important.
Style is the great illusion in art
and only man notices it
or uses it.
Still Lives
are moving us almost to tears,
to amazement.

The Roots

The roots are stretching their arms, the buds are yawning,
The sun is signalling little points of red,
There are green smells wherever you turn, the bountiful earth
Heaves and there is movement in each flower-bed.
Snowdrops seem redundant, crocuses too.
February still yet it's not hard to believe
The spring has started its labour-pains, and birth
Is taking place wherever you look or feel.
My mind stretches, I smell the tang of a new
World in time and space, and everywhere
Murder and war have left for a little while
And there's nothing but blossoming air.

It all began with a bicker,
A low note, a hopeful hint of beginnings
And I lay listening, waiting for further sounds
And they came in scores, in heralds, an orchestra
Rising now and welcoming the sun,
And the sun was spreading underneath a thin
Gauze of mist above the windows and trees,
And as the light spread and the birds' strong voices
Grew louder but no less melodious, I ran
And opened every window in my room
And my heart beat fast, my mind was open to music
And now it came in an ordered rush, a marvel
Of perfect morning. No-one spoke but the birds
And their cries were the world beginning over again
With innocence and freshness and delight,
And my eyes opened into another Eden
Sweet and unblemished, luxuriously green
And I didn't know how long I was in
A state of perfection which the birds supplied.
Then I noticed a shadow, one, and then so many
I knew that Eden could not come again
Nor I be innocent, and as sun grew
Hotter and wider I became restricted,
In bondage to a broken world within me,
But it did not matter because
I knew the overture of birds
Would happen tomorrow and draw me into its music
Soft and audacious, such a tide of voices
As never can be counted.

It is imagination's liberal side,
It is the guesswork of the intellect,
It is a metronome to which words ride
And beat their rhythms out in one swift act.

You cannot understand it if you ask
A poet. He will give approximations.
It is a gift which always means a task.
It is at best quite new illuminations.

But saying this is saying nothing much,
The poem still rides free and will not come
To easy bidding. It moves out of touch

Until it finds what did not seem a home.
Revere it but don't think of it too much.
It never will add up into a sum.

Passed Down

'I get this from my father,' one may say,
Another, 'It's my mother's fault that I
Get upset so easily.' We may
Blame many things on parents but the 'I'

Which blames or thanks, which will not claim free-will,
Is not a growing person, not complete.
We act as if responsibility
Were ours when it best suits us. Our hearts beat

Behind our ribs and signal we're alive
And have five senses of our own to choose
With every second, and we all survive

As individuals and can't refuse
How we re-act. Whatever may arrive
We've brought it on and it is marked with us.

Unsaid

I'm glad that there were some who did not speak
Their youthful love, I'm glad that I was shy
And marvelled how the heart might seem to break
Yet happily. It's good when we don't try

To urge ourselves or others to set round
Them shadows of our own. Words held me back
When I was in my teens. I heard their sound
But did not use them. Thus we learn how lack

Yields riches that no forcing will obtain.
Our first love stories are of fairyland
And maybe our last too. There is sweet pain

In thinking how we learnt to understand
Love first in little losses. Now they mean
Houses of gold which we've learnt to defend.

Katie: A Portrait

Katie has an animated face
Full of questions and discoveries,
Abounding still in childhood's easy grace,
She does not judge or bask in reveries

But fits the way the world would have her taken –
In outings to a friend, in pools of sun
Which she stands in unselfconsciously, unshaken
As yet by growing-up. Maybe she's one

Whose adolescence will not send her on
Journeys of introspection. May she have
The luck not to look inward but be one

Who will be found out by the ease of love,
Move in near-Edens where long suns have shone
And where the darker shadows seldom move.

In Praise of Anonymity

I think now of the Middle Ages when
Some clever men carved perfect gargoyles or,
In Chartres for instance, God creating man
Somewhere high up where few could see the pure

Creative fervour. No one signed his name
But was content to work with the reward
Of money only. No dark need for fame
Shadowed those artists. Their deft minds were stored

With images that owed a little to
Sermons they'd heard, bells that rang the Hours.
Who knows to what religious debts were due

Those churches which stand up today, their powers
Still vigorous? These men of long ago
Rest in kind peace beneath the spurned wild flowers.

'Music of the Spheres'

Is there a music underneath the kind
The instruments send up, conductor draws
Out of the orchestra. Is there a sound behind
The theme we hear that fills another pause

No echo eases? Maybe the ear that is
Most sensitive to sound can hear a call
Most of us miss, like heavenly harmonies
Which only on a wise, controlled mind fall.

Maybe there is and that is what is meant
By 'music of the spheres'. Perhaps each one
Of us sometimes can hear this Heaven-sent

Sound and in love that needs no words we're on
This sphere a moment. It's a grace that's leant
And is no prize for anything we've done.

Two Sonnets on Love and Lust

I

It is a person and can only be
That one, no other. So it seems at first.
Love moved with its especial melody
As if not heard before. It does not last,

Not in this kind or way, I mean. It is
A trap, a prison, lust the warder who
Locks you inside. Each touch and every kiss
Grow more insistent and it seems so true

And what you need. But you are wrong, of course,
You're caught and hardly know that this is lust.
It's passion certainly but it has laws

Love does not know of. There is little trust
But you are motivated by a cause
Which unselves you and is not kind or just.

II

How can it end? In death or loathing or
An appetite grown tired. Who has not known
This urge that uses you, is daily more
Demanding than a dream to one alone?

There is one good which grows from such a prison.
It is that love appears in its true guise,
A wishing-well united with strong passion.
When love is worked for, it's its own best prize

Ten years ago I learnt how lust could work
And it was death which brought about its end.
Mourning was terrible, most cruel and dark

And wore grey guilt. Yet grief itself could mend
The hurts and wounds of lust. Now love can lurk
And send a dove forth from its sheltering ark.

For Louise Aged 12, My Great-Niece

Louise, Louise, fill every moment now
    With hope and love,
You are upon the brink of knowing how
    It feels to change and move

About aware of being separate and
    Yourself. It will be lonely.
You have an agile mind and understand
    The natural world. Soon, only

An inward world will ask for your inspection,
    Your twelve-year body is
Lovely but you don't know its attraction.
    I wish that I could ease

The hurts of adolescence, tell you how
    Your body's changes will
Be a cause for joy. I wish I knew
    A way to keep you still

A child in many ways. Yet when I see
    You sewing, I know that
Growing may not be as it was for me
    But eager, gazing at

The world with something of the given grace
    That you possess today.
O when first love finds your unfinished face,
    May you feel joy, I pray.

My Sister

Ours is a love we never speak about,
Have never needed to. Between us lie
Two years ten days but both born in July.
As we grow older do you also feel
How rare our love is? I have little doubt
That you know well how much in me you heal.

I live alone by choice. I need to be
Alone to write. There are few friends we share.
It does not matter and we need not care.
I'm part of your own family today.
Two of your children I've known since their birth
And I remember how I used to play
With them as toddlers. Since our mother's death

I'm closer to you, understand you better.
I know that you are proud of what I write.
Do you know how your different gifts delight
Me more and more? Wife, mother, now grandmother
You are a wonder to me. Every letter
You write to me is unlike any other

Since we are blood-sisters which means we have
The gift to read between each other's lines.
We share a language shaped of little signs
We formed in early childhood. I admire
As well as love you. You can do so much
That I am clumsy at. You've taught me love
Is often richer when it need not touch.

Death of a Father who was a Poet

The father's dead. The son regrets so much
He said or did not say. He would rush back
The wasted hours when he felt within touch
And yet ignored the chance. He mourns his lack,
Wishes he were in reach

Once more and took the bold way, said the speech
He was afraid his father might flinch at.
But when one day the son feels he could reach
His stoic father, then it is too late
And now he feels too much

Guilt. He's going through his father's work
Poems as yet unpublished, and he finds
One of unusual warmth and with no dark
Reproaches. More, he learns his father's mind's
Regretful and not stark

And stoic as he thought. O time how you
Threaten family love, send quite awry
The wish and its expression. How you go
About and complicate the little shy
Feelings a man may show

To his one son who now is shedding tears
And so repeating all those arid scenes
Of cruel cross-purposes. So death appears
As almost total waste and yet it leans
Towards love. Those childish tears

The son would hide now seem an expert way
To yield and give for that one poem which
Revealed a father who had longed to say
The truth of what he felt, made death seem rich
And turned the past into a fruitful day,
With all love within reach.

A Very Great Friend and Influence

I

Finally you come because you are
    The last of friends, relations,
To whom I owe deep debts. You were a star
    To me, a constellation
That I at first looked up to from afar.
    No anticipation

Told me you would become the greatest friend
    That I have ever had.
You would be the one to understand
    All that I thought and said.
In hindsight you became a destination.
    Before we met I'd read

Much of your history and loved its grace.
    Nothing you wrote was dull.
I was excited when I saw your face,
    It was sun-burnt and full
Of life. Your voice was quick with joyfulness,
    Both kind and musical.

All of love's magic and of friendship's power
    Came from you to me.
At first I found it hard to credit your
    Friendship would one day be
The best I'd ever known. I learnt you were
    In love with poetry –

There is no other word for what you felt
    Later about my own
Poems. A mutual admiration built
    A place where we alone
Lived, it seemed. There never was a fault
    To spoil. The telephone

Almost each day brought us together. Then
    I'd read new poems to you.
I was so excited always when
    I heard your sigh, a true
Mark of your pleasure. You removed all pain
    From what cruel critics do

To poets. They possess the power to break
    A talent but you would
Heal the hurt, show me how to make
    Evil turn to good.
You spoke a spell and cast out all my black
    Faults, gave a starlight mood.

II

It is a mercy that we do not know
    The future, that I had
Never been told for sure that one day you
Would be completely lost to me, that sad

Days might come when I would wonder how
    I'd cope when you must die.
It's seven years since I have seen you now.
You are not dead but have a malady

That's almost worse. Your splendid memory
    Has disappeared. You have
Lost a great intellect which once was free
With many tongues, and now you cannot love

In any way. A dreadful illness has
    Snatched you, the most cursed
For a great writer. Do you feel distress
Now? I hope with passion that the worst

Part of the illness – I mean knowing that
    You lack your gift – has gone
And that a kind of almost-oblivion's what
You know now. May your present world be one

Such as a young child has, but more I wish
    A happy death for you.
Your spirit's gone from your once gracious flesh.
Your many friends must long for your death too.

Dear friend, kind help, dancing imagination,
    You've been dead for me long.
I treasure now your intellectual passion
But more, far more, I want you now among

Lives after-death I do not understand
    But yet hold in strong trust.
Rest soon in that believed-in holy land,
For which, great soul, you've paid so high a cost.

Was it long ago, that story,
The one that started so badly when no-one agreed,
     No-one made sense of the papers they read each morning
And we couldn't answer our children's questions? They turned
     Away and sought other guidance. It's not surprising
We failed so cruelly. We thought they were far too clever
     But not wise, and it turns out that we are the ones they trusted
Until that fell and foreign day when they went
     Not slamming doors, not arguing, not smiling
Either. They left no address. They were travelling far
     And we were staying, our unused minds were hard
And fixed. We could not imagine anything but
     What we found of ourselves in the old charged fables. We ought
To have read the messages, seen how Pandora's Box
     When opened was full of furies. We should have remembered
How dangerous the Trojan Horse was, but we forgot
     The presents we'd taken into our children's lives
Only to use them later against them. Where are they?
     Will they ever return? Will they write?
We don't deserve them. We loved them in the wrong way,
     Were now possessive, the next minute careless. O what
Is the use of regrets? We were born in a ruined age
     And we've passed it on to them
Made worse, made sicklier. So many young have no jobs
     But so many more work hard at two or three
And they give compassion and selflessness without question.
     This planet is lucky in them. They are our stars
Reflecting those others I used to love but now
     Think of them all colliding simply because of
Anger, violence, new ways of killing, new ways
     Of bruising the hearts of the young, their minds also,
But you now, David, you Peter, you Caroline, you
     Are with those who love you. Your love is rare and you give it
Out to us, donations O hampers of good,
     You love with a wisdom that shakes me. I am not worthy
Of you and you, so how can I be of God?

IN LOVE

O it is here and near. It is so sweet,
    It is the breath of spring.
It is all earlier loves and how they meet.
    It holds each happy thing

You've ever known or loved. It's wonder and
    Child's innocence again.
The world's repose, it makes you understand.
    It is delightful pain.

Fall apart, fall apart. Lie
    Together. One arm, maybe
    Touching the other's. Be
Docile and calm. Rely

On being naked in all
    The ways that are known to man.
    Sleep for the night's kind span
And praise the first bird-call.

CONTRADICTIONS

If we are arrogant and wish to be
    Solemn in all our ways,
The human body's poignant strategy
    Of sagging flesh, of hair
Thinning, limbs that falter, show our place
    In farce, black comedy.

We would be lofty, noble, dignified,
    Creatures who own the best
Of lithe, wild animals, spirits which ride
    Almost the buoyant air,
Upon this planet we think we're the blest
    Yet soil it everywhere.

We fashion shrines and temples, make the world
    Ring with angelic sound,
Write epics which are opulent and bold –
    But we shrink from the cold,
Sweat in the sun and yet make holy ground,
    And in our weak arms hold

Each other. All the acts of love we do
    Closely resemble lust.
Five senses aren't enough. We are brought low
By muscle, nerve and heart-beats. Liquids flow
    For passions' purpose, and
Yet with a simple gesture of a hand
    We show a gracious trust.

Sound it well. There is a way
To know the truth of love. It is
Much more than ways to hold and cling,
And different from seers' ecstasies.
        Mark well these words for what they say
Is – love increases suffering.

In all love's luxuries and sweets,
In all its words of honest praise
And when the sense and both minds ring
A constant round of bells, when days
        Join nights with joy, then most love meets
The realms and powers of suffering.

For when love gives much more than takes
And when the lover wants the best
For the beloved, and each frail thing
Seems wrought for lasting and shared rest,
        Such love itself makes its heartbreaks,
Is tested in pure suffering.

Since it must pass and fleetly too,
Love hears a clock and looks away
But cannot pause the hours which ring
And run swift passage through a day.
        Time is the torturer telling you
The best love means most suffering.

It was a madness of the mind and heart,
It was not shaped of sensuality
And yet it throbbed my senses, but it hurt
    My mind. It lay with me

At night, this passion that I can't explain
Even at this long distance. There was much
Joy in it but also precious pain
    And, yes, it longed to touch

But not demandingly. To see and hear
Were almost all I needed. I know now
How I was tricked and played with. I could bear
    This then, but don't know how.

I stayed quite sane when this love went away
For so he did, and he taught me obsession.
Under his cold authority I lay
    And learnt the cruelest passion.

The spell has been uncast,
   The magic gone.
The adored idol is placed
   Among everyone.

The perfect expectation
   At simply meeting
Is a routine invitation.
   The brief greeting

Is simply a shape of speech
   One can just summon up
Strength enough to read.
   Why must love stop

And the loved one only be
   Someone barely bidden?
You are back to the fatal Tree
   And the Garden of Eden.

It is a want that cannot have enough
Of what the senses give. It is a shame
That dresses up in all the trim of love,
    It is what each will blame

The other for. It seemed so sweet at first,
And so it was. None knows how it went wrong.
It was an angry hunger, baleful thirst,
    Yet it seemed to belong

To tenderness. Perhaps it started as
That, but flesh took over, making its
Demands that won't be satisfied or pass.
    This lusting always lets

You think that loving never was or could
Be kind and selfless. How does lust begin?
I only know that it's a shameful mood
    And a most deadly sin.

What ends it? Never satisfaction.
You cannot kill the senses where it works,
It is a fever and a foul infection,
    It is all shaped of darks.

MARRIED LOVE

(a sonnet for D. and A.)

They do not use the words of passion now
But they speak tender nicknames now and then.
They are familiar yet they both know how
Precious love always is and so they mean

Each word that tells of sharing. They see much
Of partings and divorce and know the worth
Of private languages and gentle touch.
Marriage makes them monarchs of the earth.

I knew a couple whom I praised for this.
They smiled and said, 'We have our quarrels though,
You must not think that everything is bliss.'

But as they spoke these words they both looked so
Compassionate, they proved that marriage is
A marvel which can somehow daily grow.

FRIENDSHIP

You need not touch, you need not feel,
    You scarcely need a sense at all
Since this love is a happy duel
    Of minds, and it is always full

Of shared excitement. Argument
    Never becomes a quarrel with
This kind of love. It is intent
    On understanding, uses breath

To share good-will, and chooses words
    That will not hurt, it moves about
And only crosses nursery swords.
    It never knows a cause to doubt

Fidelity or trust. It gives
    Unstintingly yet always keeps
Sharp eyes upon the other's griefs.
It never rests. It dares all deeps,
    It is the way the spirit lives.

It is so rare. It is unlike,
All other kinds of love we know,
    It can be like a lightning-strike
    Or come so infinitely slow.
The visionary cannot say
What this love is that takes away

All usual powers, all exercise
Of sense and flesh. It is its own
    Invader of the ears and eyes,
    It outlasts flesh and blood and bone,
My only understanding of
This gift, this ecstasy of love

Comes from what seers have told us
In words they all admit fall short
    Of both the vision and its cause.
    It does not work by cunning thought
But blesses the imagination.
It is the eighth day of creation.